>>>>>>>>>>>>>>>>>>>>>> 100% UNOFFICIAL

ROCKET LEAGUE: THE ULTIMATE GAME GUIDE

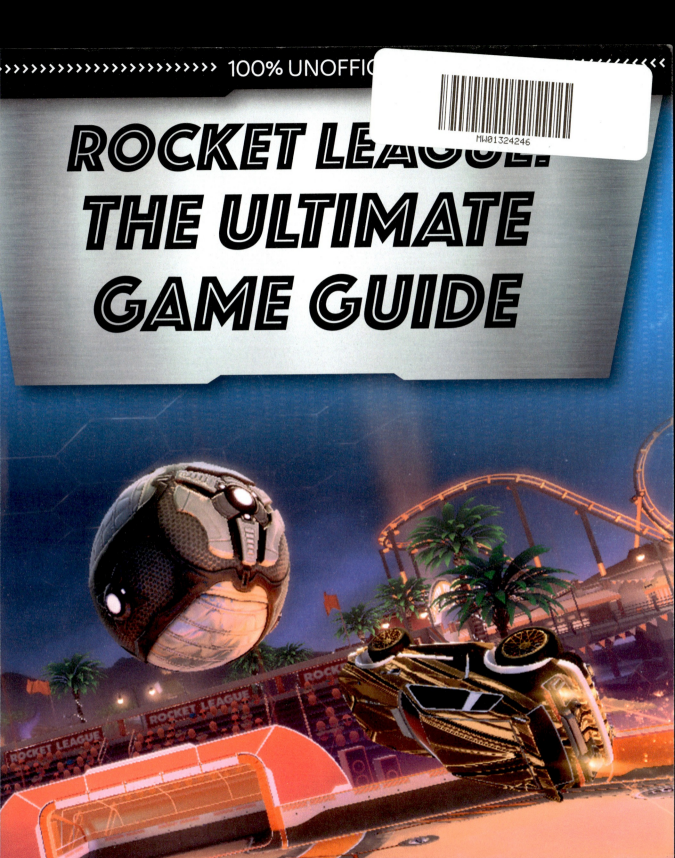

Copyright © Macmillan Publishers International Ltd 2023
Published in the United States by Kingfisher
120 Broadway, New York, NY 10271
Kingfisher is a division of Macmillan Children's Books, London
All rights reserved

ISBN: 978-0-7534-8009-0

Distributed in the U.S. and Canada by Macmillan,
120 Broadway, New York, NY 10271

EU representative: Macmillan Publishers Ireland Ltd, 1st Floor, The Liffey Trust Centre, 117-126 Sheriff Street Upper, Dublin 1, D01 YC43.

This book is not endorsed by Psyonix LLC. Rocket League is a trademark of Psyonix LLC. All screenshots and images of Rocket League gameplay and characters ©Psyonix LLC.

All information is correct as of January 2023.

Library of Congress Cataloging-in-Publication data has been applied for.

Written by Eddie Robson
Designed, edited, and project managed by Dynamo Limited

Kingfisher books are available for special promotions and premiums. For details contact: Special Markets Department, Macmillan, 120 Broadway, New York, NY 10271.

For more information, please visit
www.kingfisherbooks.com.

Printed in China
9 8 7 6 5 4 3 2 1
1TR/0323/WKT/RV/128MAA

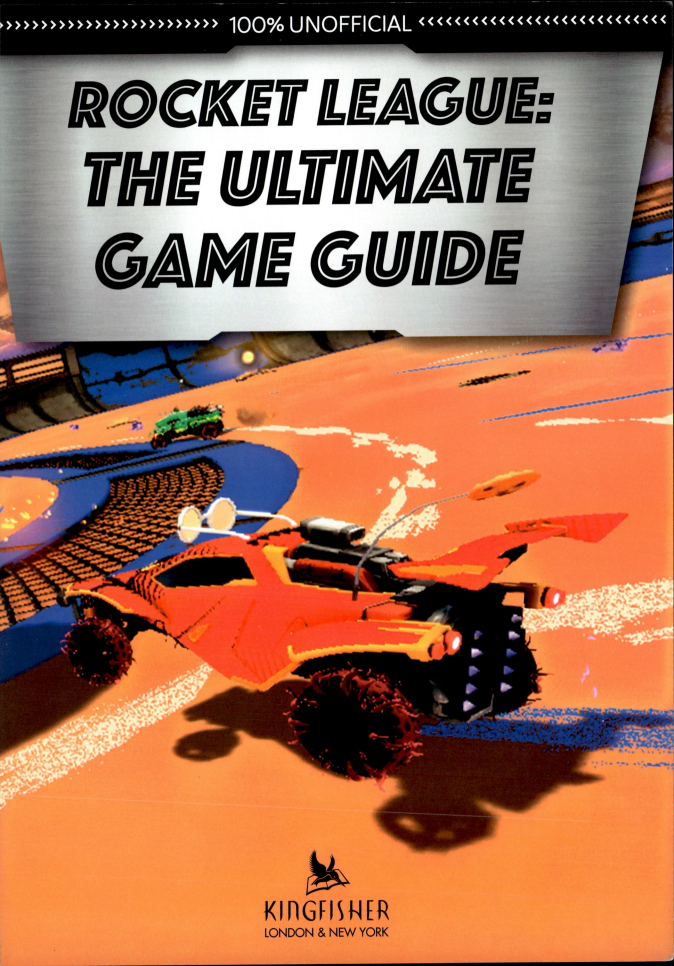

CONTENTS

IT'S NOT ROCKET SCIENCE	6
GAME MODES	10
DON'T QUIT IT	14
THE ROCKET PASS	16
IN THE GARAGE	18
HIT THE FIELD	24
ROCKET LABS	29
THROWING SHAPES	30
WINNING TACTICS	32
HOP ON THE TRAIN	34
POINT OF VIEW	36
THE KICKOFF	38

TILT AND DODGE	40
ROCKET POWER	42
JOIN THE MOVEMENT	44
UP IN THE AIR	46
KEEP ON KEEPING	48
THE BEST DEFENSE	50
DREAM TEAMWORK	52
PASS IT ON	54
DABBLE IN DRIBBLES	56
SHOOTING	58
ADVANCED SKILLS	60
THE BEST OF THE BEST	62
HAVE YOU EVER …	64

IT'S NOT ROCKET SCIENCE

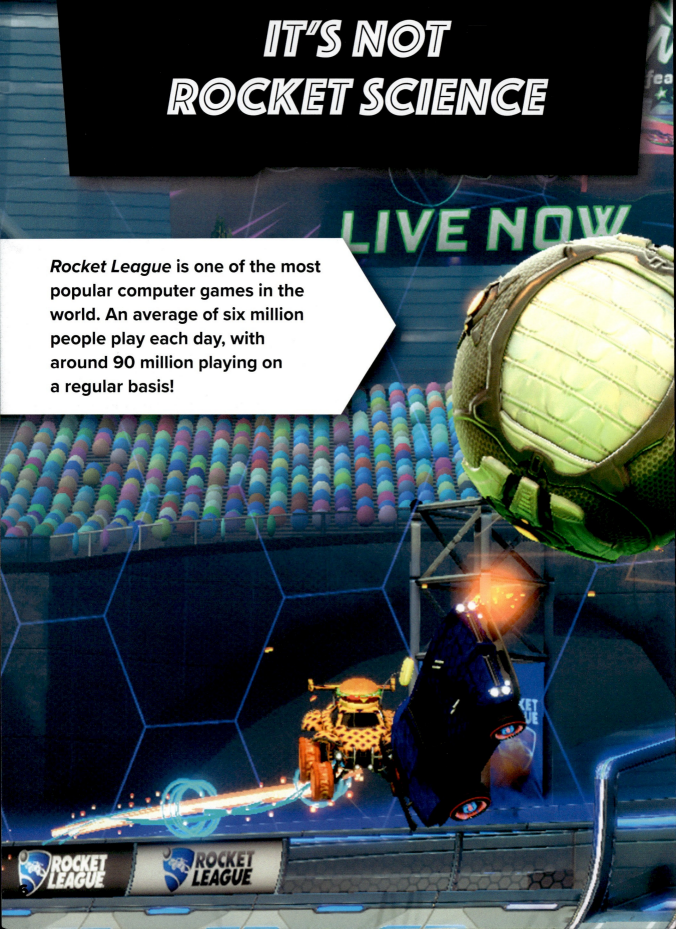

Rocket League is one of the most popular computer games in the world. An average of six million people play each day, with around 90 million playing on a regular basis!

ROCKET-POWER

It all began in 2008. Californian game studio Psyonix released a game called *Supersonic Acrobatic Rocket-Powered Battle-Cars* for the PlayStation 3, in which rocket-powered cars tried to score goals with a giant soccer ball. It wasn't a great success, but it gained a cult following among players who learned how to work with its weird physics to pull off great moves.

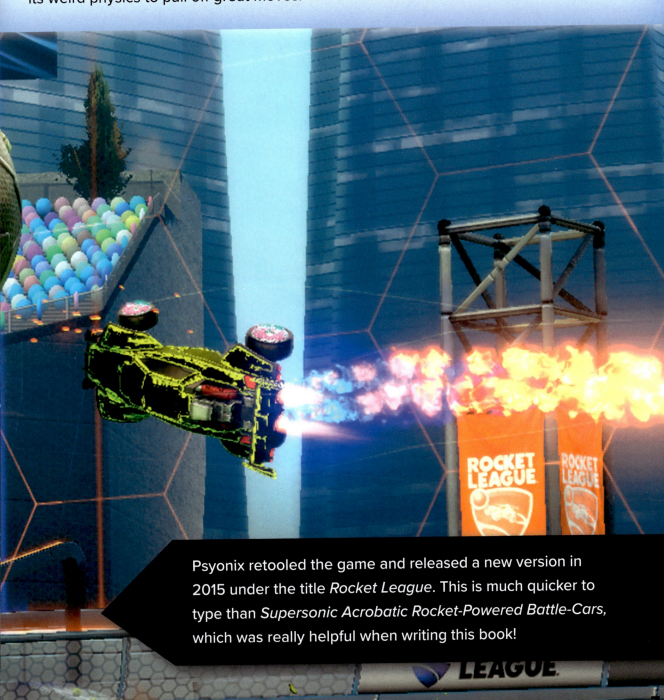

Psyonix retooled the game and released a new version in 2015 under the title *Rocket League*. This is much quicker to type than *Supersonic Acrobatic Rocket-Powered Battle-Cars*, which was really helpful when writing this book!

STAR OF THE SHOW

The physics of the game were carefully tweaked and the graphics upgraded. There were also improvements in online gaming that meant online multiplayer was now the star of the show. Lag problems had been much reduced, and players could find a game to get involved in at any time of the day or night. This was a huge part of what made *Rocket League* a hit, and it was soon released for all major platforms.

Rocket League and esports were a perfect fit, and in 2016 Psyonix launched the *Rocket League* Championship Series. This tournament now has a prize pool of over two million dollars!

FREE-TO-PLAY

In 2019, Psyonix was purchased by Epic Games (makers of *Fortnite*), and the following year *Rocket League* went free-to-play with a similar model to *Fortnite*. Gameplay is divided into seasons, and each of them has a **Rocket Pass**—revenue is generated from cosmetic items sold in the shop. So you don't have to pay a thing for *Rocket League* if you don't want to!

GAME MODES

DIFFERENT WAYS TO PLAY...

In **Competitive** online play, you have a ranking that will improve if you win matches and drop if you lose. How much you go up or down is balanced against the quality of your opponent—in other words, if you lose to better players, your ranking will drop less than if you're beaten by lower-ranked players.

COMPETITIVE

3v3
STANDARD

2v2
DOUBLES

1v1
DUEL

PLATINUM — SEASON REWARD LEVEL

1/10 WINS — MUST BE DIAMOND RANK TO ADVANCE

There are 23 tiers of Competitive play, ranging from **Unranked** all the way to **Supersonic Legend**, and within each tier there are four divisions—that's a massive ninety-two tiers you can go up or down!

As you'd expect, **Casual** online play is more relaxed. It doesn't matter if you win or lose since there's no official ranking, but the game will monitor everyone's results and try to put players of equal ability together. So Casual is good if you just want to have fun and try out some new moves, or if you don't want the stress of having to protect your ranking.

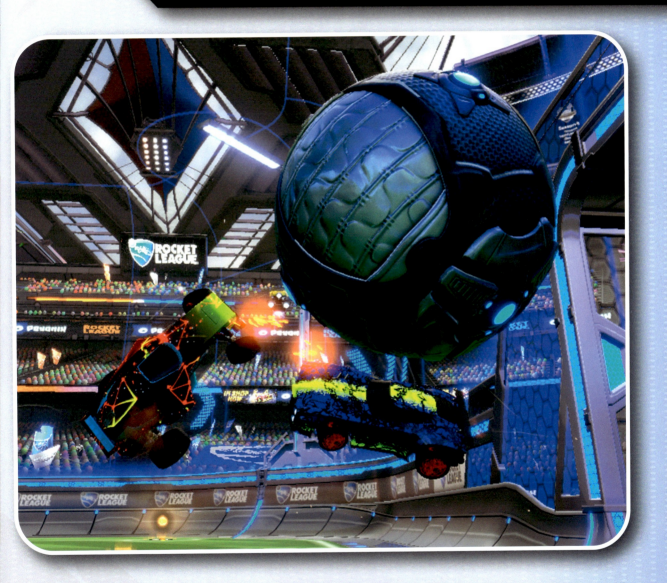

In both Casual and Competitive, you can play **Standard** (three players per team), **Doubles** (2v2), and **Duel** (1v1). Competitive also allows you to play **Rumble**, **Dropshot**, **Hoops**, and **Snow Day**. Casual doesn't have those, but it does have **Chaos** (4v4) and limited-time modes (LTM).

Some of *Rocket League*'s game modes offer something a little different from the standard soccer-style game.

RUMBLE

This game mode sticks with the soccer format but adds *Mario-Kart*-style power-ups. For example, the **Spike** power-up covers your car in spikes that make the ball stick to it, while **Magnetizer** draws the ball toward your car. **Power Hitter** means harder strikes of the ball but also instant demolition of opponents!

HOOPS

This tricky game mode is based on basketball, with hoops replacing the goals. But unlike basketball, you can't hold and throw the ball—so this is a bit like trying to play basketball with your feet. You need to develop skills like jumping to flick the ball upward when it drops near the hoop and dribbling the ball up the walls.

SNOW DAY

In this, the usual giant soccer ball is replaced by a giant hockey puck with different physics—the puck will usually slide rather than rise into the air, which means you won't need as many aerial moves. The arena you play in will always be a snowy variant.

| 3v3 RUMBLE | 3v3 DROPSHOT | 2v2 HOOPS | 3v3 SNOW DAY |

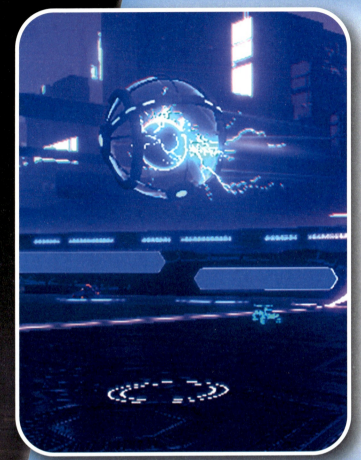

DROPSHOT

Instead of scoring goals, in this mode players must create holes in the floor on the opposing team's half and then push the ball into them. Each hexagonal panel is destroyed after the ball hits it twice. The more times the ball is hit by a vehicle without touching the ground, the more charged it becomes. In its second phase of charge the ball damages all the surrounding panels, so one hit damages seven panels. In the third phase the ball damages a further ring of panels, meaning 19 panels will be damaged in one hit!

LIMITED TIME MODES

Sometimes **LTMs** are introduced with different rules to the regular game—some of them are **battle modes** that don't even use a ball. Play them while you can!

DON'T QUIT IT

YOU COULD GET FROZEN OUT...

Players quitting matches early while losing used to be a constant feature of *Rocket League*, which would force the game to replace them with bots or draft in new players looking for a match. To stop players doing this, matchmaking bans were introduced. Getting one will freeze you out from joining new online matches for a limited period.

KEEP IT CASUAL

When you know you may get interrupted and have to leave a match early, play Casual. You can leave one Casual match per day without a ban, but your second early exit will give a ban of five minutes, while the third will give a ban of ten. If you're only leaving matches because you have to, rather than because you're losing, this shouldn't be a problem. Even if you get a ban, it'll only be short and will probably be over by the time you've dealt with whatever pulled you away from the game.

If you quit a Competitive match early, you'll be warned not to. If you go ahead, you'll incur a ranking penalty and receive a matchmaking ban, which starts at five minutes for the first quit and goes up to 24 hours for the seventh. So even if you're losing, play to the end!

DO YOUR OWN THING

It's also possible to play offline against bots, or there's local multiplayer where you can actually set up private matches against friends. There's a **Free Play** mode in Training that puts you in an empty arena with a ball to test out moves and tactics. All good uses of your time if you get a matchmaking ban!

THE ROCKET PASS

GET MORE OUT OF THE GAME...

The **Rocket Pass** is an incentive to play the game more regularly by offering limited-time rewards to players. Each season of *Rocket League* has its own Rocket Pass, and new seasons launch every few months.

You can still earn items from the Rocket Pass without paying for it. Accessories for your car like **toppers**, **paint finishes**, **antennas**, and **wheels** can be earned at certain tier levels, or you might be able to pick up **titles** and **banners**. You can also acquire drops of increasing rarity as you go up the tiers, which will grant random items.

Pay for the **Premium Rocket Pass**, and you can earn everything from the free track, plus more desirable items like car bodies, XP boosts, and credits.

The most important thing to remember about the **Rocket Pass** and the other items you can buy in the game is that none of it gives you an advantage in matches. They either change the look of your car, jazz up your profile, or give you an XP boost. You can't buy an advantage in *Rocket League*—that only comes from getting better at the game!

CREDIT WHERE IT'S DUE

You can use credits to buy items from the shop, trade items with other players, or build items by using blueprints. You can even hang onto them to buy the next Premium Rocket Pass. You can earn up to 1,000 credits by working your way through the game.

PLAYING WITH FIRE
LIMITED TIME
-65%
2000

CYCLONE BUNDLE
LIMITED TIME
-65%
500

MEAN GREEN
LIMITED TIME
-70%
1100

AUDACIOUS MOVES
LIMITED TIME
-44%
1000

INSIDIOUS ORANGE
LIMITED TIME
-60%
1100

CREEPED OUT
LIMITED TIME
-58%
500

IN THE GARAGE

MAKE YOUR CAR YOUR OWN!

At the **garage**, you can choose:

BODY The type of car.

PAINT FINISH Teams are divided into Blue and Orange, but here you can select different shades of each. You can also choose to be green or purple when you're on Blue, and yellow, red or pink, when you're on Orange.

DECAL A design you can add to the car's body.

TOPPER An object placed on top of the car—often a hat but sometimes something even sillier!

ANTENNA A decoration for your car's radio antenna, such as a flag or small toy.

19

WHEELS

Tires of different thickness, different rim and hubcap designs.

ROCKET BOOST

What comes out of the back of your car when you use boost.

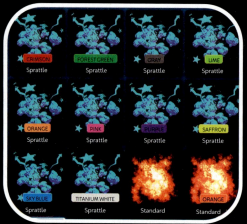
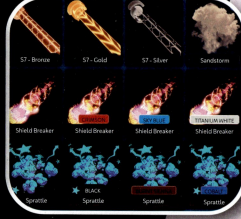

TRAIL

Like **Rocket Boost**, but it only appears at supersonic speeds.

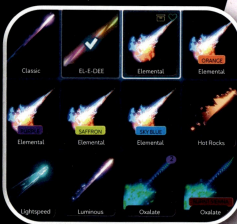

GOAL EXPLOSION

The ultimate flex—these appear in the opponent's goalmouth after scoring.

ENGINE AUDIO

The sound of your engine—which can be a great way to annoy opponents.

> You can also change your **Title**, **Player Banner**, **Avatar Border**, or **Player Anthem** here.

You start off with a limited selection of items, but you can unlock more by completing matches and reaching new tiers on the Rocket Pass. For new players, the only car bodies available will be **Breakout**, **Merc**, and **Octane**, but you can unlock another eight default bodies—**Backfire**, **Dominus**, **Gizmo**, **Hotshot**, **Paladin**, **Road Hog**, **Venom**, and **X-Devil**.

21

New car bodies are being introduced to *Rocket League* all the time. However, the important thing to understand about car bodies is there are only six types of **hitbox**, and every car in the game belongs to one of those categories.

The **hitbox** is how the game defines the outer edges of your car when it comes to hitting the ball, hitting other players, or coming into contact with any part of the arena. It doesn't matter what the car looks like, the hitbox is what makes the difference in how a car plays—and there's at least one default freely available car for each type.

Here are the six types of hitbox:

BREAKOUT

Examples of this type include **Breakout**, **Animus GP**, **Cyclone**, **Komodo**, and **Nexus**.

BREAKOUT

HYBRID

Venom and **X-Devil** are default Hybrid types. Other Hybrids include **Esper**, and the **R3MX**.

VENOM

MERC

This bulky model is the least frequently used. Beyond **Merc**, it's also the hitbox for **Nomad**.

MERC

Pro players tend to favor **Octane** and **Dominus** models. The Octane is best for accurate shooting, and the Dominus is best for power.

OCTANE

Here's a popular one and the basis of several default cars, including **Octane**, **Backfire**, **Gizmo**, and **Road Hog**. **Outlaw**, **Proteus**, **Scarab**, and **Takumi** are also **Octane** models.

PLANK

Paladin is the default Plank model. Others include **Artemis**, **Mantis**, **Sentinel**.

DOMINUS

This is another of the most popular body types. Beyond as the default options **Dominus** and **Hotshot**, this is used for a lot of the tie-in cars and real-life vehicles. The **Guardian** and **Chikara** ranges are also **Dominus** types.

BACKFIRE

MANTIS

DOMINUS

HIT THE FIELD

A QUICK TOUR OF THE STADIUMS...

Earlier versions of *Rocket League* featured arenas of different shapes, but the play area has now been standarized. This means the main arenas only differ in appearance and are all rectangular. The non-standard versions are still available to play but can't appear in **Casual** or **Competitive** playlists.

AQUADOME

An underwater arena where your matches are witnessed by fish as well as a crowd.

BECKWITH PARK

This is like a community field in a public park. It's based on a real park where *Rocket League* level designer Ben Beckwith used to play as a kid!
VARIANTS: Stormy, Midnight, Snowy

Watch out for limited-time arena variants, which often appear as tie-ins. The Bat-signal could be seen above Beckwith Park when *The Batman* was released, while Farmstead was moved to the Upside Down to coincide with a new season of *Stranger Things*!

OPEN AIR

Some arenas are open to the air, while others are enclosed rooms. But this doesn't make a difference to gameplay because the open-air ones have a forcefield grid.

DEADEYE CANYON

At this crowdless arena in the desert, there are curious details in the background, such as a tiny Stonehenge.

DFH STADIUM

This is one of the most popular arenas in the game and was named after David F. Hagewood, Psyonix's CEO. The Circuit variant places a racing track around the edge.

VARIANTS: Snowy, Stormy, Day, Circuit

CHAMPIONS FIELD

This is a huge modern stadium where the default is nighttime.

VARIANT: Day

FORBIDDEN TEMPLE

This East-Asian-styled arena situates its goals underneath ornamental bridges.

VARIANTS: Day, Fire & Ice

MANNFIELD

This and DFH Stadium are the two possible locations for the Championship match in Season mode.

VARIANTS: Night, Stormy, Snowy

FARMSTEAD

Located out in the country, this field has small stands and goals made of corrugated iron.

VARIANTS: Night

NEO TOKYO

This arena resembles Akihabara—Tokyo's famous electronics and geek-stuff district.

VARIANT: Coamic

NEON FIELDS

Released to coincide with the music-themed *Rocket League* Season 2 in 2020, this has the look of an outdoor music festival.

SOVEREIGN HEIGHTS

Although similar in style to Beckwith Park, this arena is set in an urban location instead.

STARBASE ARC

This sci-fi arena, which is in orbit around a planet, replaced an octagonal version when the arenas were standardized.

VARIANT: Aftermath

UTOPIA COLISEUM

A funky take on classical architecture, this arena has some attractive tiling around its goals.

VARIANT: Dusk, Snowy, Gilded

RIVALS ARENA

This is quite similar to Championship Arena, but it was redesigned for a partnership with Hot Wheels. It is a standard arena, but it doesn't appear in online playlists.

SALTY SHORES

A new rival to beach volleyball emerges with this seaside arena.

VARIANT: Night

WASTELAND

Play rocket-car soccer in a post-apocalyptic landscape for the full *Mad Max* vibe.

VARIANT: Night

URBAN CENTRAL

A classy arena that uses architecture you might see in a train station built around the turn of the 19th century.

VARIANTS: Dawn, Night

ROCKET LABS

GET A LITTLE EXPERIMENTAL!

Unusual, original layouts find their home in the Rocket Labs section. Some of these stadiums feature different shapes, while others include obstacles on the field. And some have been developed into fully designed arenas—the **Octagon** arena was the prototype of **ARCtagon**, while **Underpass** became **Tokyo Underpass**.

When Rocket Labs was first introduced, it included a fixed collection of arenas. However it's now a limited-time mode, and when it reappears as an online playlist, it features different arenas. You can still select all the arenas for local or private matches, and some of them appear in the Rumble game mode.

UTOPIA RETRO

is circular and the two goalmouths are positioned back-to-back.

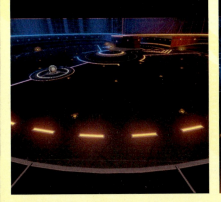

COSMIC

is especially tricky because the sides of the arena are all raised, including the goals.

DOUBLE GOAL

creates two goalmouths by placing a pillar in front. Any ball that passes into this extended goalmouth area is a goal.

THROWING SHAPES

FOR A SLIGHTLY DIFFERENT GAME, TRY THESE NON-STANDARD ARENAS...

ARCTAGON

This is the original version of Starbase ARC. Its octagonal shape means that it has eight full-boost pads (rather than six), with one at each point of the octagon.

BADLANDS

This used to be Wastelands, and it's striking because the sides of the arena slope upward toward the walls.

VARIANT: Night

THROWBACK STADIUM

This is based on a stadium from *Supersonic Acrobatic Rocket-Powered Battle-Cars*. It has a goal line that extends into the arena so players can move behind the goal, like in hockey.

VARIANT: Snowy

TOKYO UNDERPASS

Formerly Neo Tokyo, this is a split-level arena with an upper floor running along each side. Moving between the levels can be tricky!

Hoops mode uses the **Dunk House** and **The Block** arenas, while Dropshot takes place in **Core 707**. Snow Day always takes place in the Snowy variant of **DFH Stadium** or **Utopia Coliseum**. Knockout takes place on three special arenas, which are **Calavera**, **Carbon**, and **Quadron**.

PLAYING FAVORITES

Increase the chances of getting put into a match in your favorite arenas on online playlists by using **Arena Preferences**. On this screen, you can choose which arenas you like or dislike. If everyone in a lobby dislikes an arena, then it won't appear. If some dislike it, it'll have a lower chance of appearing. But if more like an arena, it'll have a higher chance of appearing.

WINNING TACTICS

ROCKET LEAGUE IS SIMPLE, WHICH MEANS THERE ARE MANY DIFFERENT WAYS TO APPROACH IT.

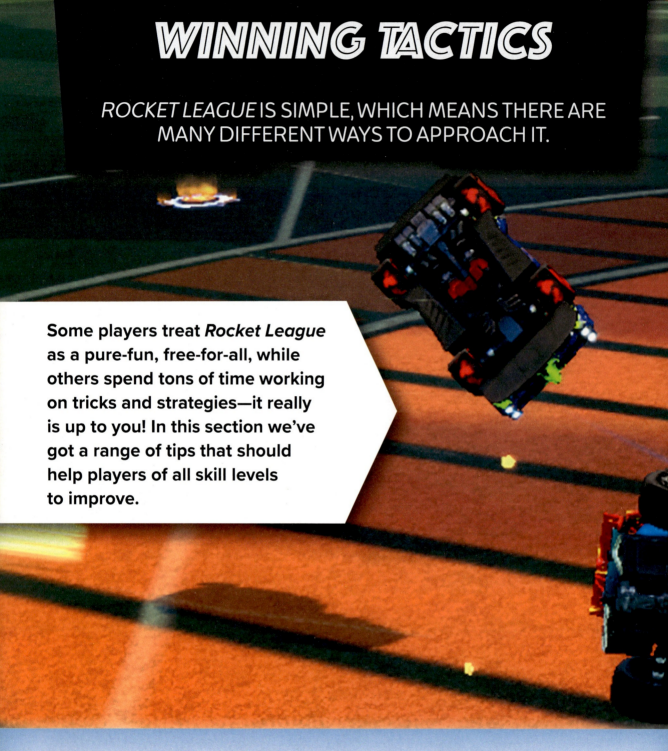

Some players treat *Rocket League* as a pure-fun, free-for-all, while others spend tons of time working on tricks and strategies—it really is up to you! In this section we've got a range of tips that should help players of all skill levels to improve.

Besides as useful advice that might change how you approach the game, there are also obscure tricks involving the physics of the game—these have become super popular among the more skilled members of the *Rocket League* community.

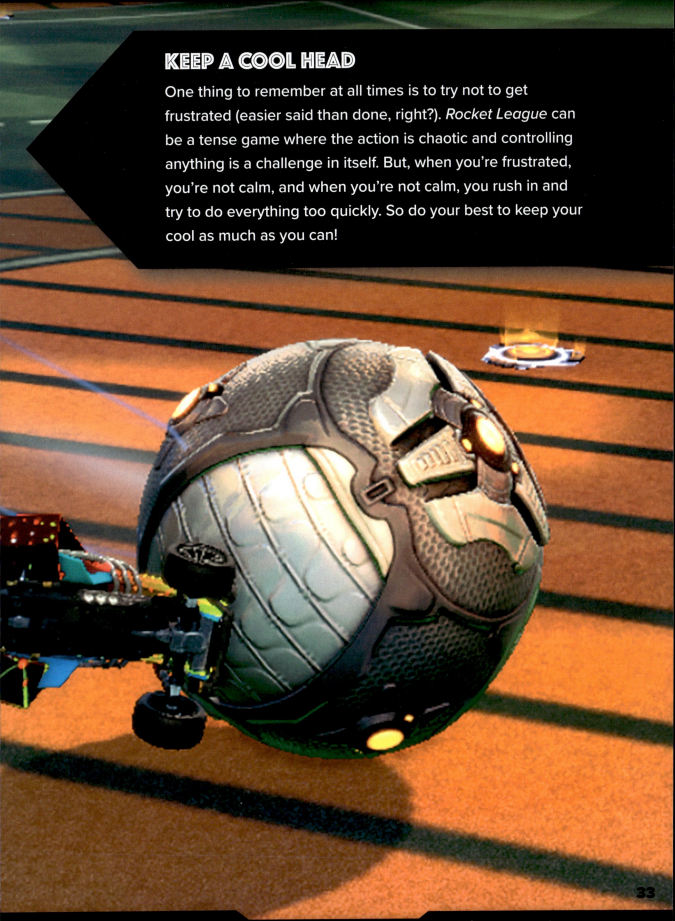

KEEP A COOL HEAD

One thing to remember at all times is to try not to get frustrated (easier said than done, right?). *Rocket League* can be a tense game where the action is chaotic and controlling anything is a challenge in itself. But, when you're frustrated, you're not calm, and when you're not calm, you rush in and try to do everything too quickly. So do your best to keep your cool as much as you can!

HOP ON THE TRAIN

GET THE BASICS DOWN FIRST. ONCE YOU'VE NAILED THOSE, THERE'S LOTS MORE YOU CAN LEARN!

If you're new to *Rocket League*, do the introductory tutorial before you try to play a match. If you've played before but haven't done the tutorial, we suggest you go back to it (it's in the Play section under Training.)

TIME TO TRAIN

Unless you're really, REALLY good at the game, a few minutes spent at the training ground is always worthwhile. In the heat of a match it's easy to fall back on simpler moves and ones you know you can execute, but training may show you something you didn't know how to do or had forgotten you can do.

CUSTOM TRAINING

There are plenty of routines that many players never touch. Besides as programs on particular aspects of the game (Aerial, Goalie, and Striker), there are **Custom training programs** made by Psyonix and top players. Some of them are mega challenging—how to execute a particular shot within a very short time limit can be more of a puzzle than a test of skill—but they're always worth trying out.

FREEPLAY FUN

If you want to get good at a particular skill—whether it's dribbling, aerial boost, or side flips—freeplay is the place to do that. Duck in there while you're waiting for the game to find a server, or if you're sitting out a matchmaking ban. And sometimes it can be fun to take the competitive element out of *Rocket League* and just enjoy it.

GO SOLO

If you want to hone your skills, try playing 1v1. You may find it kind of boring and annoying having to chase down every ball and roll it into the goal yourself. However, take some time to play 1v1 and you'll come out of it a better player.

POINT OF VIEW

KEEP YOUR EYE ON THE BALL.

One of the biggest talking points for players is **Ball Cam**—the view that keeps the ball in the center of the camera. Experienced *Rocket League* players often recommend using it, but a lot of beginners find it too hard and go back to the standard **Car Cam**.

ON THE BALL

The tricky thing about Ball Cam is that you're not in control of the camera. You constantly have to adjust your direction, and if you're not driving toward the ball, you can't always see where you're going. Keep using the Ball Cam, though, because you will get used to it—and you'll find it easier to make contact with the ball and time your shots correctly.

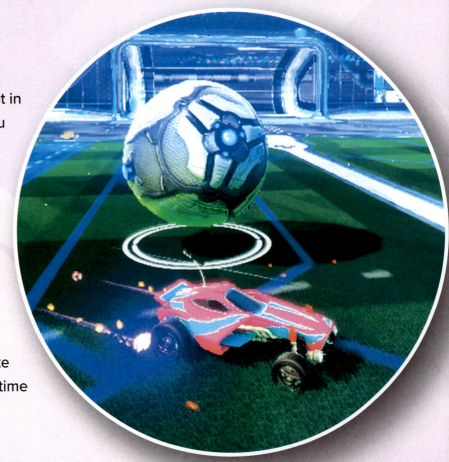

EASY REACH

The Ball Cam toggle control is easily accessible for a reason. Picking up boost can be annoyingly difficult with Ball Cam, and demolishing other players is also tricky. So if that's what you're looking to do, just turn off the Ball Cam and turn it back on afterward. The same applies if the ball is hanging high in the air and you want to see what's going on around you instead of looking up at the ceiling.

> Certain moves with the ball benefit from turning off Ball Cam. Changing direction while dribbling can be hampered when your view is locked onto the ball. If you're doing a flick with a side roll, you may not want the camera to move. But you do need a bit of experience to do those well anyway, so it's best to make Ball Cam your default.

WHAT'S YOUR ANGLE?

There are lots of different options in the camera settings. Pro players recommend turning camshake off. Everyone's preferences are different, but start off by trying an FOV of 110, a low angle such as -3, a distance of 270, and a height of 110, then tweak it until you find what works for you. Play with the swivel speed, too—it goes up to 10, and if you can take in the view quickly when you move the camera, the max setting may be best.

THE KICKOFF

GET THINGS RIGHT FROM THE START WITH THESE CENTER-CIRCLE TIPS.

At the kickoff there are five possible starting positions—**left** and **right wing**, **left** and **right defense**, and **goalkeeper**. If you're in one of the defensive positions, use the seconds before the kickoff to swing the camera back and check if a teammate has spawned in the goalie position.

GOALIE DEFENSE

The player in the goalie spot is the furthest from the ball. But they also have the straightest angle on it, and with more boost pads between themselves and the ball, they can get there first. So you can let them go for it, but one of you should stay back to defend in case a shot comes in.

BOOST IT

Start yourself moving with a hit of boost, but don't use it all—after you've collected the first boost pad in your path, use a forward flip. Then apply more boost to reach the ball. Finally, use another forward flip as you reach the ball—this will apply more force to your contact and will help block the ball if your opponent reaches it first. Aim to hit the ball dead center.

VARY YOUR APPROACH

Everyone loves those direct-from-the-kickoff goals, but a decent team won't give you those opportunities. At lower ranks, watch for those chances and take them, but trying to shoot every time isn't always the best strategy! If the opposition keeps winning kickoffs, try angling your first touch differently. And you can vary your approach by using **side flips** and **diagonal flips** as you make contact with the ball—or something between the two, known as a **corkscrew flip**. Flips are also good for generating power, and with the corkscrew flip, you can boost into the ball.

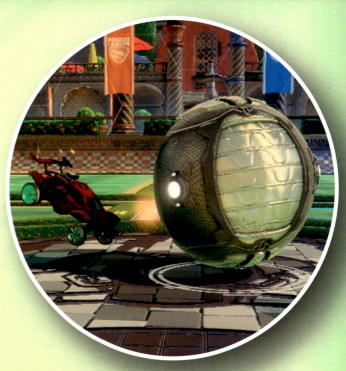

HIGHER LEVEL APPROACH

More advanced players can speed flip to launch themselves at the start of the kickoff (more on how to speed flip later!). At higher levels you may see other players doing this and reaching the ball first every time. Don't worry—in most cases you can still reach the ball and block whatever your opponent does. Learn to watch your opponent's approach so you know how to counter it.

> Players spawning on the wing may prefer to duck out of the kickoff, pick up a max boost pad, and then follow up whatever their teammates are doing. Just make sure someone goes in for the ball!

TILT AND DODGE

YOUR CAR IS A BIT OF A BLUNT INSTRUMENT, BUT THERE ARE SOME SUBTLER MANEUVERS AVAILABLE.

TILTING

When jumping, you can tilt your car forward or back. Each will have a different effect when you hit the ball. Tilt back before you make contact, and the ball will hit your wheels, bouncing more gently. This can be good for **tap-ins**, as it avoids the ball bouncing up off your hood and missing a target. If you tilt the car forward so it bounces off your roof, it should angle the ball down. This is a good tactic when meeting high balls, because otherwise you may just hit them even higher. It's also necessary to perform the **Flip Reset**, but more on that later. . .

SIDE DODGING

Side dodges or side flips are covered in the advanced tutorial. They involve jumping, then jumping again while pressing in a sideways direction. This move can be used to nudge the ball into the goal from close range, to make a save or for a quick **course-correction** when you are trying to hit the ball and realize that you're going wide.

MUSCLE MEMORY

It can be tricky to get the hang of using tilt and dodge in a match when you only have a split second to choose a move, so they're one of the best things to practice in freeplay. Build muscle memory and learn to execute them instinctively. Advanced players can use them as part of a planned maneuver rather than to adjust position in the air, but this means you need to anticipate where the ball is going and where the dodge will take you.

ROCKET POWER

USE YOUR BOOST… BUT DON'T OVERUSE IT!

Unsurprisingly, **rocket boost** is a big part of successful *Rocket League* play. Scoring goals is hard without boost unless you have an open goal. And when you get back to defend, the field feels very long without boost. So don't use it unless you have to, and don't hold down the boost button every time you use it. A few little speed bumps can be just as effective.

BOOST PADS

It can be tempting to prioritize chasing after **boost pads** when you're low, but don't let it pull you out of the match! If you study the patterns of the regular boost pads and get used to taking those paths up and down the field, you can pick up plenty of boost without going out of your way.

TRICK SHOT

Similarly, using up boost pads can be a good way of frustrating opponents. Using a little boost to drop your own levels below 100% just before you hit a max-charging boost pad can leave it empty for your opponent. Just try not to steal it from your teammates, too!

WAVE BOOST

After jumping you can hit jump again with "up" and it'll make you flip and hurtle forward. You can achieve speeds similar to your boosted speed by doing this, which is known among players as **wave boost**. Use it if you're all out of boost, or better yet, use it to conserve boost for when you really need it. It's possible to cancel the flip and still get the speed boost. Jump, tilt your car back a little—and then, just before your back wheels touch down, hit jump and up. If you're close enough to the ground, the flip should push your front wheels onto the playing surface and cancel the flip.

ON THE FLIP SIDE

The **forward flip** is easy and incredibly useful! If you don't already use it, build it into your play. It's good for getting extra height or gaining some quick momentum when you're standing still. You can also use it to get extra power on shots. If you hit the ball with your roof, it can help to keep the ball on the ground.

JOIN THE MOVEMENT

THE MORE CONTROL YOU CAN GET OVER YOUR MOVEMENTS, THE BETTER.

Watch a world-class soccer player like Lionel Messi, and you'll see how comfortable he is with changing up the speed of his play. He'll wrong-foot defenders by slowing down, then speeding up again. The same is true of *Rocket League*. Being able to slow down your play and switch direction will make you a much better player.

POWERSLIDE

If you're not using your **powerslide** just as much as jump and boost, you're not using it enough. It has a much tighter turning circle than driving forward, which means you turn faster and don't have to travel out of your way to do it. You can use it to make 180-degree turns or to turn at right angles. It can be super effective if used along with reverse when you need to get into position.

8-BALL

It's a good idea to keep moving since you need to be in motion to jump and turn effectively. But you don't want to be chasing after the ball all the time, especially if your teammates are doing that already! So if you're lurking in the middle of the court while teammates are attacking, try doing figure eights over the same spot. This keeps you moving and means you can quickly launch in one direction or the other—whether it's to join the attack or head back to defend.

ROLL WITH IT

But there's an even quicker way to change direction if you find yourself facing completely the wrong way. Jump and tilt your car as if you were going to land on your roof—but roll while in the air and land on your wheels.

UP IN THE AIR

THE BALL SPENDS A LOT OF TIME IN THE AIR—DON'T JUST HANG AROUND WAITING FOR IT TO COME DOWN.

There's a training routine to help you time aerial shots—do this and practice it. The **Beginner** version has a static ball for you to hit, but the **All-Star** version is what you need to master if you're going to pull off good aerial shots in matches. And of course, this skill can come in handy when defending or fighting for the ball in the center of the arena.

AIR CAM

Aerials are one part of the game where it can be better not to have **Ball Cam** on because you need to be thinking about where the ball is going next, not where it is at that moment. However, Ball Cam can also help you stay on target. If you do keep Ball Cam on, bear in mind there's always something above the goal that will help you locate it when you're in the air. Most stadiums have marker lines extending upward from the goalposts, while others such as Farmstead have struts that are in line with the goalposts. These markers are helpful if the ball is much higher than the goal, and you can't keep both in view at once.

AIR ROLLING

When you're in the air, pressing left or right will usually make your car spin around horizontally. To make it roll, hold down the powerslide button. This can be a handy move to put yourself the right way up while falling. You can change the sensitivity of your air roll controls depending on how skilled you are. Set them too high, and you'll lose control of the car, so try nudging them up a little at a time until you find the right setting for you. An advanced tip is to side dodge one way while air rolling in the other—this is tricky to master, but it can enable you to defy gravity!

KEEP ON KEEPING

INCREASE YOUR CHANCES OF AN EPIC SAVE.

In real-life human soccer, when the goalkeeper is facing down an opponent, they will usually prioritize covering the near post (the one the opponent is nearest to). However, in *Rocket League* you need to move forward for an effective save, so a bit of reaction time is helpful. This means the near post might not be the best place to be. By the time you react and move forward, the ball might have passed you and be heading for the goal.

KEEP WATCH

For this reason, it can be better to defend from the far post, especially if you're staying still and watching an attack, waiting for it to develop. From there you can move across the goal to make saves and use that space to adjust your position as you move. A lot of goals go in above the height of your car, so a little space to jump into is helpful in saving those.

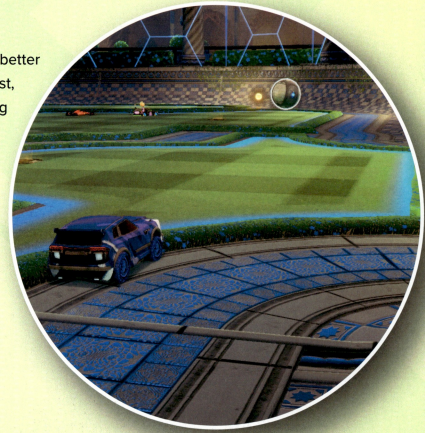

PRIME SPOT

Similarly, in real-life soccer it would be a terrible idea for the goalkeeper to stand well behind the goalline. But in *Rocket League,* this is another way of giving yourself extra time and space to move forward when you see the ball coming. So if you're the last line of defense, position yourself inside the goalmouth at the far post.

CROSS SAVES

Making saves by going across the goal, rather than blocking shots head-on, will also send the ball out to the side. If the ball is traveling slowly, a simple block may send it rolling loose in the penalty area, leaving a free shot for an opponent.

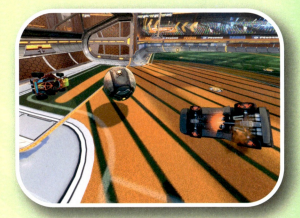

Remember that advanced players will look to avoid the ball rebounding from the backboard above the goal, so it won't drop into the penalty area. If your aerial game is good enough, knock these balls to the side, too.

THE BEST DEFENSE

THERE'S NO NEED TO BE SO DEFENSIVE. OH WAIT, THERE IS!

As a general rule, one player on each team should be defending at all times (or at least ready to go back and defend). This is why 3v3 is the default mode of *Rocket League* so that one player can defend while the other two try to link up to score. You can either have one player focus on defending all the time, or you can rotate the role. The chat option "Defending . . ." comes in handy here.

SIMPLE SYSTEM

If your whole team is back defending, try using a rotation system. This involves picking three spots that your team will move between. Imagine the ball is on the left-hand side of the court. The first spot will be in front of the goal, the second can be the maximum boost pad in the left corner, and the third can be the right-hand side of the penalty area.

BE READY

Starting at the goal, head out to the boost pad and try to clear the ball or demolish opponents. If you fail to do so, head for the right-hand side of the area, where you can block or demolish opponents waiting for a cross, or be ready to pick up the ball if it goes across the goal without going in. Now move back to your starting position in the goal, so you're ready to make a save.

The benefit of this tactic is that if one of you fails to clear the ball, a teammate is always following up, and your other teammate is taking their place in the goal. So with just three players, you can create waves of defense. It involves coordinated teamwork, but if you have a regular team you play with, it's a tactic worth trying.

DREAM TEAMWORK

LINK UP THE PLAY!

You can use a **rotation system** when attacking, too. One player can position themselves by the max boost pad on the halfway line, a second by the max boost in the corner on the same side, and a third in the penalty area.

The first player should be trying to pass to the second player, who should be trying to pass to the third player. If the pass doesn't work out, the first should head to where the second player is, the second should head to where the third player is, and the third should rotate back to the first position.

CHANGE ROTATION

However, this means leaving your own goal unattended, and a high-level opponent will punish you when you lose the ball. If you're playing a team who'll likely send the ball forward if you fail to score, use a different sort of rotation system where you head back toward the goal after your job is done.

IT TAKES THREE

The first player takes the ball up the field (probably along the sideline and collecting boost in the process) and tries to pass or score. . . if they get the chance. The second takes up a more central role (a little behind the first player) and looks to get on the end of the pass and score. The third comes in a little behind that and looks to collect the ball if the striker misses or to follow up a saved shot.

KNOW YOUR PLACE

All three should be ready to rotate back into defense after their job is done. The third player can try to keep the ball at the other end or pass back to their own player. But if the opposition gets the ball and starts an attack, the first player should be back defending the goal.

PASS IT ON

YOU DON'T GET A FREE PASS IN THIS GAME.

Passing is the cornerstone of real soccer, the most important thing to be able to do well—but this isn't real soccer! The lack of precision in *Rocket League*, as well as the fact that you have fewer teammates, makes successful passing very difficult.

STARTING RANK

At lower ranks, passing isn't really an option. Most players will just hit the ball in the direction of the goal and hope that, if it doesn't go in, a teammate is there to snap up the rebound. Or they'll bounce the ball off the walls and try to send it into the danger area. This is a totally legit way to approach the game up to and including **Platinum** rank.

PASSING RANK

As you get better, you may have the confidence to play **back passes**—just make sure you're not doing it in the direction of your own goal. Also, make sure there's a teammate to pick up the ball so it doesn't just go into space. This can work well if one of you stays back in your own half to defend. If the player making the pass attracts one or more defenders to their position, their teammate can exploit the space left and move into attack. The one who made the pass can then rotate into defense.

RANK UP

Further up the ranks you'll encounter players who are very sound in defense, and passing can help you play past them. This is all about making your play less predictable since high-ranked players will be able to defend well in a one-on-one situation. So if you can roll the ball sideways into space, or deliberately send it rebounding across the penalty area, a teammate may have an open goal. Just make sure you know where your teammates are!

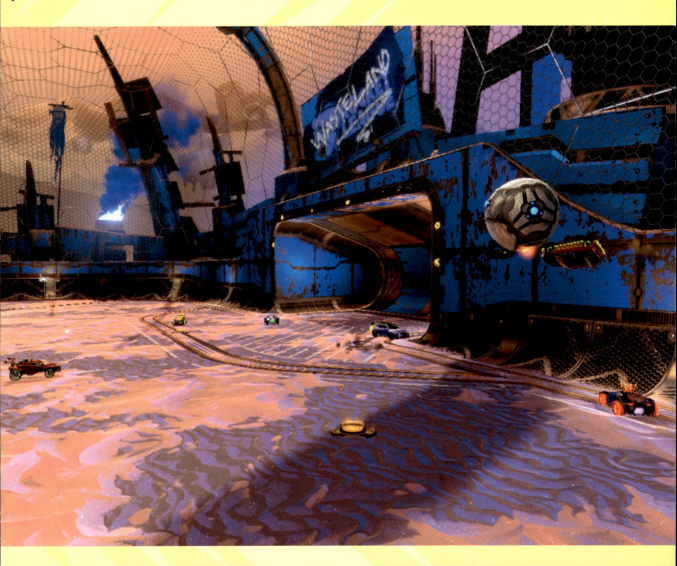

Voice chat is a huge help. A teammate can use it to tell you if they're set up to take the shot or not. Even if you can see them moving into position, they may be all out of boost!

DABBLE IN DRIBBLES

CLOSE CONTROL ISN'T EASY IN THIS GAME...

Sometimes you get a chance to carry the ball in space. If you're not a good dribbler, it's tempting to avoid using boost so you can keep better control. But this is easy to defend against—opponents will have time to get back, and goalkeepers will have time to prepare.

FEATHER THAT BOOST

The trick is to **feather** the boost, using a little at a time. If you use too much boost, you'll end up with more momentum than the ball, and you'll find yourself sliding under or around it. This is a great thing to practice in freeplay or, better yet, in 1v1.

ALL IN THE ANGLE

Less experienced players will only dribble when the opportunity presents itself—when the ball has fallen to the ground and stopped bouncing. But you can create your own dribbling opportunities by practicing a first touch that angles the ball down and doesn't send it shooting away too far. Try tilting the car to help with this.

CARRY ON

It's also possible to carry the ball on the hood of your car rather than doing a soccer-type dribble where the ball travels in front of you. For that, you definitely need to turn off **Ball Cam**. When you're close to the ball, give it a little boost—just enough to carry you into the ball. Now you need to feather your boost really carefully. The white circle on the ground that shows the ball's position is your friend here—don't look at the ball, just keep your car in the middle of that circle. With a well-timed flick, you can send the ball toward the goal or into the danger area.

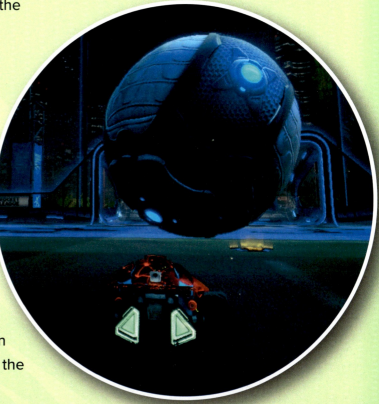

SHOOTING

HOW TO SCORE MORE!

The direction of the ball affects the power of your shot. If it's coming directly at you, some of your power is already being used up by reversing the direction of the ball. It's easier to use the momentum of the ball and add to it if it's coming across the face of the goal, and you're trying to redirect it at a 90-degree angle.

ULTIMATE POWER

The most powerful contact you can make with the ball is by using the corner of your **front bumper** because this concentrates all the momentum of your approach into a single point. Imagine a line going from the opposite back corner to the corner of the front bumper—this is the ideal line to be traveling on as you hit the ball.

ON THE NOSE

In practice, it's not always going to be so simple to line up a shot that way, and the nose of your car will be an easier way to make the shot. But try flipping and angling your car just before hitting the ball, so you make the final contact with the corner. However, accurate shooting is more important than maximum power! Remember to angle your car to direct the shot.

GOOD GOLLY, HALF VOLLEY

There are four basic types of shot: **ground shots**, **volleys** (hitting a ball as it drops), **half volleys** (hitting a ball after it bounces), and **aerials**. Aerials are a more advanced technique, but the half volley is a great one to practice. The difference between this and a volley, is that the ball is already travelling upward when you hit it, whereas on a volley the ball is traveling down. If you hit a half volley the moment after the ball bounces directly at the goal (rather than adding more upward momentum), you can produce a shot with a speed and height that makes it very difficult to save!

ADVANCED SKILLS

THINK YOU'RE PRETTY GOOD? TRY THESE TECHNIQUES...

SPEED FLIP

This move used to be **elite** level but has become more and more common. Flipping gives you a speed boost, and you get the most power from the corner of your front bumper. Here's the best way to get that boost while keeping your car on that angle!

After jumping, press up and a little to one side while jumping again. This will send you into a slightly diagonal forward flip. Next, cancel the flip by pressing down and a little to the same side and keep holding that as you hold air roll to control your movement. On a console controller this involves very quickly moving your thumb from jump to air roll, so a lot of players bind air roll left and right to the L1 and R1 buttons. This move takes practice to master, but it can really transform your game!

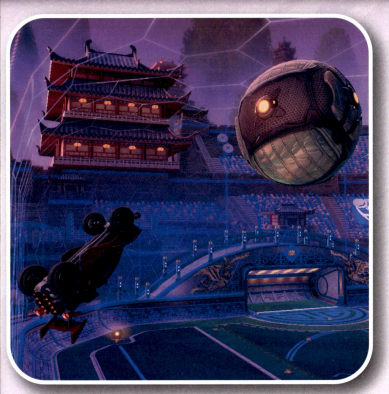

AIR DRIBBLE

If you're confident in the air and have mastered the on-the-hood dribble, you can try this. With a gentle boost into the ball when it's in the air, you can push the ball forward while not sending it ahead of yourself. Feather the boost and try to match the speed of the ball, so it neither drops nor goes too far ahead. This is very, very tricky, but it's also mega difficult to play against!

FLIP RESET

This is one of the most advanced moves in the game and is only for players with good aerial control. You'll be aware that cars can flip themselves in the air once per jump to gain extra height. This is reset when the car's wheels touch a surface—usually the ground. But the surface of the ball also counts! So, if you tilt your car back as you make contact with the ball, you can flip again and keep your car in the air. This works well with the speed flip. Master this move, and you can make multiple touches of the ball without ever touching the ground!

THE BEST OF THE BEST

Professional *Rocket League* esports is getting more competitive all the time. Let's look at some of the world's top teams and their star players . . .

TEAM BDS

France has always performed well in *Rocket League*. The all-time top earner, Alexandre Courant aka Kaydop, is French—and Swiss-based Team BDS has assembled a spectacular roster of French players. Their superstar is Evan "M0nkey M00n" Rogez! Many consider him the best *Rocket League* player in the world, and he's often found at the top of the doubles rankings. BDS trounced G2 Esports 4-1 in the best-of-seven series to claim the 2021/22 World Championship.

OCTANE: TEAM BDS (AWAY)
VERY RARE DECAL

NRG ESPORTS

The USA-based NRG is one of the biggest names in esports, and *Rocket League* is at the heart of their success. The team was already performing well when they signed Garrett Gordon (GarrettG), in time for Season 3 of the World Championship Series. This addition took their game to a new level and brought them their first Championship in 2019, with Season 8. GarrettG is the only player to have reached the Championship Series every year since it began!

FENNEC: NRG (AWAY)
VERY RARE DECAL

G2 ESPORTS

German-based G2 Esports have tasted considerable success with their North American team, winning the Winter Split Major in 2022. They may have missed out on the 2021/22 World Championship, but their confident run to the final suggests a strong future with players such as Canadian Jacob "JKnaps" Knapman.

FENNEC: G2 ESPORTS (AWAY)
VERY RARE DECAL

FAZE CLAN

American outfit FaZe Clan are relatively recent entrants into the *Rocket League* world, having signed the entire roster of The Peeps in 2021. However, all three members of that team were quickly replaced, and FaZe Clan's star player is now Jason Corral, known as Firstkiller. Two regional titles in his first year, plus a top-four showing at the World Championship, shows it was the right move.

OCTANE: FAZE CLAN (AWAY)
VERY RARE DECAL

HAVE YOU EVER...

CHECK OFF EACH EPIC MOVE AS YOU DO THEM.

- [ ] SCORED A HAT TRICK
- [ ] MADE AN EPIC SAVE
- [ ] BEEN MVP IN A MATCH
- [ ] SCORED WITH A SIDE DODGE
- [ ] SCORED USING WAVE BOOST INSTEAD OF ROCKET BOOST
- [ ] SCORED A HALF VOLLEY
- [ ] WON A SNOW DAY MATCH
- [ ] WON A HOOPS MATCH
- [ ] WON A MATCH IN EVERY STADIUM IN THE CASUAL / COMPETITIVE PLAYLIST
- [ ] COMPLETED THE BEGINNER AERIALS TRAINING DRILL
- [ ] DONE A SPEED FLIP
- [ ] DONE A FLIP RESET